THE SECRET WORLD OF

Crabs

THE SECRET WORLD OF

Crabs

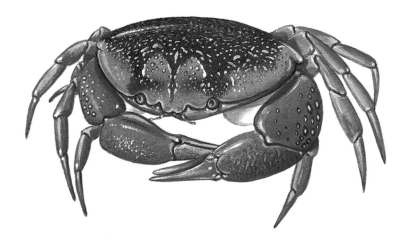

Theresa Greenaway

RSVP RAINTREE
STECK-VAUGHN
PUBLISHERS

A Harcourt Company

Austin   New York
www.raintreesteckvaughn.com

Published by Raintree Steck-Vaughn Publishers, an imprint of Steck-Vaughn Company

Acknowledgments
Project Editors: Sean Dolan and Kathryn Walker
Illustrated by Colin Newman
Designed by Ian Winton

Planned and produced by Discovery Books

Library of Congress Cataloging-in-Publication Data

Greenaway, Theresa, 1947-
Crabs / Theresa Greenaway.
p. cm. -- (Secret world of--)
Includes bibliographical references (p.).
ISBN 0-7398-3506-8
1. Crabs--Juvenile literature. [1. Crabs.] I. Title.

QL444.M33 G75 2001
595.3'86--dc21

00-062833

Printed and bound in the United States
1 2 3 4 5 6 7 8 9 LB 05 04 03 02 01

Contents

CHAPTER 1
Curious Crabs

 The largest crab is the giant spider crab from Japan. Its chelipeds span 11 feet, 10 inches (3.6 m), and its body is about 15 ½ inches (40 cm) across.

 The heaviest crab is a fully grown giant crab from the sea near southern Australia. Its body is about 17 inches (43 cm) across, and it weighs 33 pounds (12.4 kg). Out of water, its claws are too heavy for it to lift.

 The sand-dollar peacrab is one of the smallest crabs. Its tiny body only reaches one-quarter inch (5 mm) in length.

 The horseshoe crab is not a crab at all. It is much more closely related to spiders and scorpions.

Crabs belong to a group of animals called crustaceans. Their closest relatives are shrimps, prawns, and lobsters. Like insects and spiders, crustaceans are arthropods. All arthropods have a hard body covering, or exoskeleton, and several pairs of jointed legs. It is easy to recognize a crab. It has a short body that is often wider than it is long and two big pairs of pincers, or claws, held out in front.

A crab's body has a head, thorax, and abdomen. The head and thorax are merged together under a hard shell called a carapace. Crabs have five pairs of legs attached to the thorax. The two front legs, called chelipeds, each bear a pair of pincers. Behind these are four pairs of walking legs, each with a pointed foot. At the rear of the thorax is the crab's abdomen, which is no more than a small flap in most crabs.

There are more than 4,500 different species, or kinds, of crabs. They are divided into two groups, a large group of true crabs and a smaller group containing hermit crabs, porcelain crabs, and king crabs. True crabs have small, flat abdomens that are folded up against the underside of the thorax. There are no tail-like flaps at the tip of this abdomen. Hermit, porcelain, and king crabs do have tail-flaps. Although the abdomen of porcelain and king crabs fold flat against the thorax, hermit crabs have long, unfolded abdomens and live inside the empty shells of sea snails.

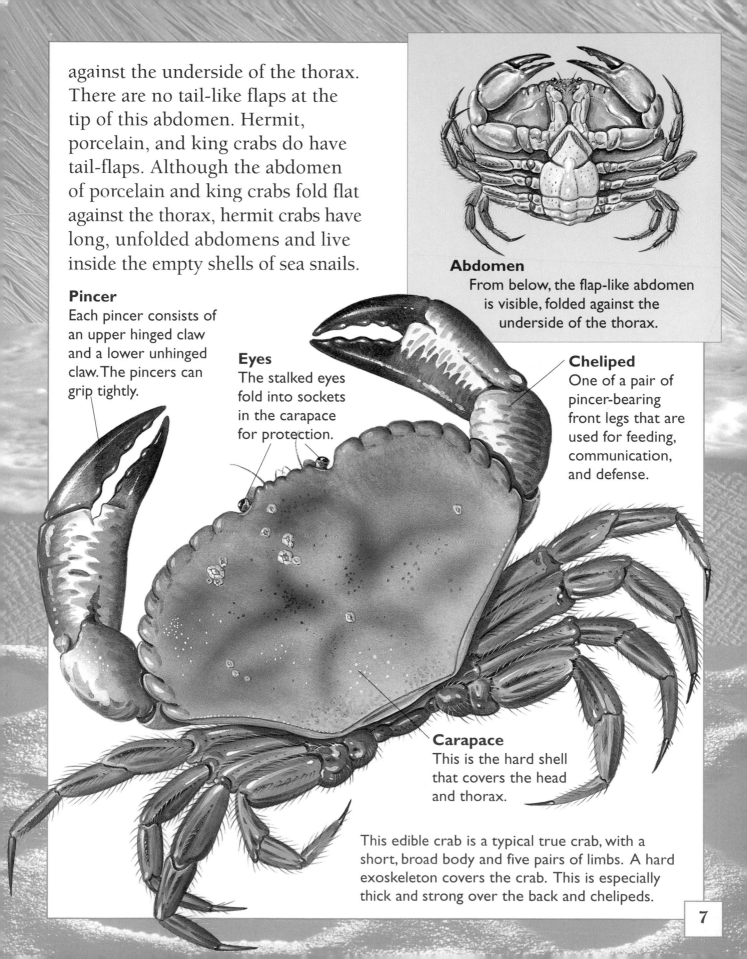

Abdomen
From below, the flap-like abdomen is visible, folded against the underside of the thorax.

Pincer
Each pincer consists of an upper hinged claw and a lower unhinged claw. The pincers can grip tightly.

Eyes
The stalked eyes fold into sockets in the carapace for protection.

Cheliped
One of a pair of pincer-bearing front legs that are used for feeding, communication, and defense.

Carapace
This is the hard shell that covers the head and thorax.

This edible crab is a typical true crab, with a short, broad body and five pairs of limbs. A hard exoskeleton covers the crab. This is especially thick and strong over the back and chelipeds.

Most crabs live in the sea, from the shoreline down to the deepest parts of the ocean. Shoreline crabs are covered by salty water or exposed to the air as the tides come in and go out. Storms may send huge waves crashing down, so crabs and other shore wildlife must be able to cling to rocks or take shelter. In deep water, the conditions are more stable, but there may be fewer places to hide.

Some other kinds of crabs, for example, like the Chinese mitten crab, live in fresh water. Others

▲ In spite of its extremely long, spindly legs, the giant spider crab walks quite slowly over the seabed.

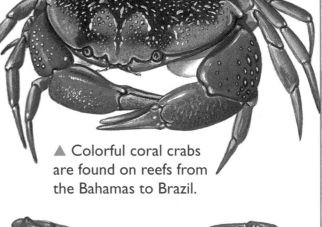

▲ Colorful coral crabs are found on reefs from the Bahamas to Brazil.

▲ An adult Chinese mitten crab lives in freshwater rivers but has to travel to the mouth of the river to breed.

spend at least part of the day on land, and some, such as the mangrove crab and the soldier crab, spend most of their time on land. To avoid drying out, land crabs hide somewhere damp during the hottest part of the day.

▲ This tropical land crab digs down and makes a cavity in damp soil in which to spend the day.

HEAD

At the front of a crab's head there are a pair of stalked eyes. Slightly below these are two pairs of feelers, or antennae. The crab's mouth lies below these. The mouth of a crab is made up of pairs of hard mouthparts, which have different uses. A pair of jaws hold the food; other structures pull bits off and put them into the crab's mouth. A flap on one pair of these mouthparts pumps water over the crab's gills, so the crab can breathe.

An impressive array of hard mouthparts processes the crab's food before it is finally swallowed.

CRAB SHELL

The whole body of a true crab is covered and enclosed by a hard outer layer of cuticle called an exoskeleton. This layer is made of protein and a chalky material. The cuticle covering the crab's back and its chelipeds is especially thick. This hard, shelly outer layer protects the crab from wear and tear and also helps to protect it from enemies. Thinner, more flexible cuticle covers the joints of the legs, so that they can bend. A crab's hard shell cannot stretch, so in order to grow, the old shell is shed from time to time. This is called molting.

A crab's hard shell also contains colored pigments that give each species its characteristic color and pattern. The light-colored markings on the carapace of this lined shore crab help identify it.

Hermit Crabs

A hermit crab has a hard layer of cuticle covering the front part of its body and its legs, but its long abdomen is soft. Hermit crabs live inside the empty shells of other animals, usually those of periwinkles, whelks, and other marine snails. The curved abdomen fits snugly inside a coiled snail shell, and the two tiny tail flaps grip the tip of the shell firmly. A hermit crab also grips the rim of its shell with its last two pairs of walking legs. When a hermit crab grows too big for its shell, it has to find a larger one.

BREATHING

Most crabs can breathe only in water. Delicate, feathery gills on each side of the thorax absorb oxygen dissolved in the water. The gills are hidden under the sides of the carapace, which forms a chamber over them. Water enters the gill chamber through tiny holes between the legs. It is wafted over the gills and leaves the chamber through openings just above the mouth. Fiddler crabs store water so that they can breathe for some while before returning to water, and land crabs breathe air.

CHAPTER 2
Crabs in Motion

 Ghost crabs can run forward, backward, and sideways at speeds of up to 4 miles (6.4 km) per hour.

 The mangrove tree crab climbs 33 feet (10 m) or more to the tops of mangrove trees.

 The large land crab digs 3 feet (1 m) deep burrows 4 inches (10 cm) across, with a small chamber at the bottom where the crab can keep cool and damp during the day.

 The mud crab digs a burrow with an emergency exit. Its U-shaped burrow has two main entrances and sometimes side tunnels as well.

Why do crabs walk sideways? There is a very good reason for this—the long walking legs are so close together on each side of a crab's short body that if it were to move forward, the legs would trip over each other. By scuttling sideways, this is avoided. Many kinds of crabs, such as the Sally Lightfoot, can sprint over sand or rocky ground extremely quickly. Crabs can walk on land as well as over the seabed, or submerged rocks.

As well as walking on land or under water, some kinds of crabs use their legs to burrow into the ground under the seabed, and some are surprisingly good at climbing. How they normally get from place to

Like other crab sprinters that need to move quickly across open spaces, this Sally Lightfoot crab has large, prominent eyes to detect predators.

Swimming crabs are flattened and have a light carapace to help them move speedily through the water. The shell of this swimming crab is covered with tiny sea animals called hydroids.

place depends largely upon where they live. Many kinds of crabs live on rocky shores. Those such as the king crab are slow-moving crabs with a thick, heavy shell and large, powerful pincers. Their short legs enable them to cling tightly to rocks and to haul themselves through seaweed or into sheltered rock crevices. Crabs that live in exposed places with little shelter, such as muddy or sandy beaches, are sprinters. Ghost and fiddler crabs need to be able to run quickly back to their burrows when danger threatens.

SKILLFUL SWIMMERS
Most crabs are able to propel themselves through water, but the swimming crabs excel at swimming. These crabs need to be able to swim quickly to catch the fast-moving fish they eat. They have large eyes to help them see their prey. Designed for speed, swimming crabs have light shells and slender legs. The last pair of legs are flattened into paddles that can be used both to move the crab forward and to send it darting sideways through the water. The carapace of the blue crab has a long spine on each side so that it is even more streamlined for sideways swimming.

CLIMBING CRABS

Most crabs can clamber over rocks and debris underwater, but some are equipped to scale beds of waving seaweed or large reefs. Spider crabs and coral crabs are strong climbers with feet that can grip tightly so that even strong waves do not dislodge them. On land, crabs such as the rocky shore crab and the mangrove tree crab also have feet that enable them to maintain a grip on trees and branches.

sideways. Back-burrowing crabs, such as mole crabs, sit on the sand, lean backward, then dig into the sand with their legs until only their eyes or antennae can be seen. Some of these burrowers are able to dig very rapidly and make a new burrow every time they need to hide.

This crab keeps a firm hold on the tree trunk by pushing its feet into cracks in the bark.

BURROWING

The only place to shelter on a sandy seabed or beach is under the sand or mud itself. Burrowing crabs either burrow backward or

Crabs that live partially or completely on land, such as fiddler, ghost, and mud crabs, excavate more permanent burrows, which may be just simple upright tunnels of about 6 inches (15 cm) or more complex, branching burrows. These crabs are side-burrowers.

Robber Crab

The robber crab of the South Pacific and Indian oceans (also known as the coconut crab) is well-known for its habit of stealing anything that takes its fancy. Amused observers have watched robber crabs making off with items such as wristwatches, cans, sandals, and cutlery! Robber crabs are also excellent climbers. They can climb 66 feet (20 m) or so up a smooth palm tree trunk to feast on its fruit.

Using the legs on one side of its body, the crab digs out soil or mud and carries it in balls to the entrance. These burrows last for many weeks; the crabs retreat into them when the tide comes in or whenever they are threatened. They plug the entrances with a mud lid.

The ghost crab races back to its burrow at the slightest chance of danger. Its long-stalked eyes fold sideways into its shell when it is safely underground.

CHAPTER 3
Crab Senses

 Ghost crabs have the best eyesight—they can see a large moving object at about 330 feet (100 m) away.

 A crab detects food under water by using its senses of smell, taste, and touch.

 Tiny sense organs at the base of each antenna let the crab know which way is up and help it to keep its balance in air or water.

 A ghost crab's eyes are wrapped right around its eyestalks, so the crab has 360° vision.

Crabs have senses of sight, touch, taste, and smell. They can also detect vibrations in water, and some can also detect vibrations transmitted through the ground. Some kinds of crabs, including ghost and fiddler crabs, can hear. A crab's senses help it to know what to do and when. They help it to detect a predator so that it can escape from danger and help it to find food, a mate, and the right place to live.

The velvet swimming crab lives among rocks in shallow coastal waters. By day it stays sheltered in a rock crevice, but when it detects increasing darkness, it emerges to feed.

A crab's senses also tell it when the time is right to come out of its shelter, and when to return. In the sea, most crabs are active at night. Swimming crabs, walking crabs, and spider crabs all emerge at night to hunt and feed. As day breaks, these crabs return to shelters under rocks or in burrows.

Shore crabs have another cycle —the twice daily tides. The common shore crab, or green crab, comes out to feed at high tide. When the tide falls, it hides in tide pools or under seaweed. It will come out at high tide during the day, but it is most active at high tide at night. Fiddler and ghost crabs hide when the tide is in and only emerge as it goes out. Many of these kinds of crabs are most active during daytime low tides.

EYES

Crab's eyes are on the tips of stalks, and they fold into sockets in the carapace for protection. Having eyes on stalks means that a rather flat crab has a better field of view. Crabs have compound eyes, just like insects. Each eye is made

A ghost crab uses its eyes to spot moving prey as well as larger predators but relies on its sense of smell to discover other food items such as carrion (dead animals).

up of thousands of small units, each with its own tiny lens. Compound eyes do not give a clearly focused image but are very sensitive to movement and can see colors. Eyesight varies from species to species, and it is less important to some kinds of crabs than others. Slow-moving, heavily armored shore crabs rely on strength rather than speed and therefore have small eyes.

Life in the Deep

The deep sea crab lives at about 8,200 feet (2,500 m) in warm water vents in the eastern Pacific Ocean. It is completely dark at this depth, so this crab is totally blind. It finds its prey of worms and deep-sea clams by smell and the vibrations these animals make in the darkness.

A SENSE OF TOUCH

In spite of their hard shell, crabs have a good sense of touch. This is because growing through the cuticle are tiny but very sensitive bristles. These touch-sensitive bristles are scattered all over a crab's body, and there are many of them on the legs and feet. Other types of hairs are sensitive to vibrations traveling through the water. These hairs are found mostly along the pincers.

CAN CRABS HEAR?

It is not yet known whether all crabs can hear, but scientists have discovered that ghost and fiddler crabs certainly can. These crabs make special sounds to attract mates or warn off rivals. Some sounds are made as the crabs rub or vibrate their legs. They make other sounds by tapping the mud or sand with their pincers. To detect these sounds, the crabs have "ears" inside the tips of their legs. These are small, flat sheets of cuticle that work somewhat like the eardrum in each of your ears.

TASTE AND SMELL

Crabs can smell things to eat underwater by detecting chemicals from food with the tufts of hairs on the tips of their antennae. When a crab detects these chemicals, it starts to search for the food by moving in the direction where the smell is strongest. Taste-sensitive hairs are located on the mouthparts, along the pincers, and on the crab's feet. When the feet touch something edible, these hairs tell the crab to pick it up with its claws and start eating.

Different kinds of hairs and bristles on a crab's antennae, mouthparts, pincers, and the rest of its legs are sensitive to touch, taste, and smell, so a crab can find food even in the dark.

CHAPTER 4
Food and Feeding

Most crabs are happy to eat almost anything, plant or animal, dead or alive, that they come across. Animals that have such a wide range of food items in their diet are called omnivores. Such crabs will seldom go hungry. They will always manage to find something to eat. Other crabs are more fussy in their eating habits, but even so, in times of need, they too will eat whatever is available.

Predatory crabs use their pincers to catch their prey, and all omnivorous crabs catch or forage for their food and pick it up with their pincers. Each pincer is made up of an upper, hinged claw and a lower, unhinged claw. The hinge

A hungry shore crab will catch and eat another crab if it can overcome it, and it will also eat dead crabs.

 A pair of brand-new sneakers belonging to a biologist studying crabs on Christmas Island were snipped, shredded, and then carried away by a robber crab!

 Robber crabs take turns to snip their way through coconut shells and feed on the white coconut inside.

 Mangrove crabs will try to eat anything—they will even sneak up to a rat and grab its tail!

 Land crabs eat mostly plants but will devour a dead animal if they get the chance.

 Freshwater crabs add fish and frogs to their menu when they can catch them.

A dead fish is an easy meal for a crab. This Sally Lightfoot crab is snipping off pieces of flesh with its pincers and passing them to its mouthparts.

allows the upper claw to move to and fro so that it can grip. The jointed parts of the rest of the cheliped allows the crab to reach in all directions with its claws.

The shape and size of these claws varies from species to species. Most have saw-like teeth along the edge of one or both claws. These help the crab to grip its food, and in some species, such as robber crabs, these teeth are sharp enough to cut up hard food such as coconuts. Most crabs use their claws to pull apart their food and pass pieces of it to the jaws. These

jaws hold onto and bite the food, so that the next sets of mouthparts can shred it and pass it into the crab's mouth.

PREDATORY CRABS

Swimming crabs are able to catch fast-moving fish or prawns because they can dart through the water quickly and snatch their victim using their slender, sharply toothed claws. Heavier crabs such as the edible crab, cannot catch such active prey. These largely carnivorous, or flesh-eating, crabs feed instead on worms, slow-moving starfish, and mollusks, such as mussels, whose shells they can crush with their strong pincers. They also dig their prey out of the sand with their pincers.

SCAVENGERS

When the tide goes out, it leaves a line of debris along the shore. The debris includes strands of dead seaweed, dead seabirds, dead fish, pieces of wood, and all kinds of trash that has either been thrown from ships or washed down rivers and into the sea. Tiny invertebrates such as sand hoppers and small flies swarm all over it. Crabs and other animals forage among this debris, a manner of feeding called scavenging.

These land hermit crabs are scavengers, feeding on anything edible that they come across. Here, they are eating the debris that collects in the cracks in a piece of driftwood.

FILTER FEEDING

The action of waves helps to break up dead animals and dead seaweed. The larger particles sink, but the smaller ones float. Seawater also carries bacteria and other tiny living organisms. Animals that get their food by straining these tiny animals and floating particles from the water are known as filter feeders. A few crabs get their food in this way. The mole crab has feathery antennae that trap tiny particles of food from the water. These are scraped off by the pincers into a pellet of food, which is then put into the mole crab's mouth.

Food from Mud

The fiddler crab and the sand-bubbler crab (pictured here) leave their burrows when the tide goes out to feed by straining particles of plants and animals from the exposed shore. Clawfuls of mud or sand are scooped into their mouths, where the mouthparts separate out the edible particles and spit out the rest as round pellets.

SCRAPING A LIVING
Underwater rocks and corals are covered with a layer of tiny marine organisms. The pincers of spider crabs, such as the red spider crab, end in ridged, spoonlike tips that are used to scrape off this nutritious layer. The mouthparts are hairy, which prevent the crabs from dropping these small particles.

CHAPTER 5
Competitive Crabs

 Up to 500,000 young king crabs cluster together to make gigantic heaps on the seabed.

 Crabs that start a dispute are usually larger than their opponent and therefore more likely to win.

 A defeated blue crab lets its opponent know it has won by folding its claws close against its body and crouching low on the ground.

 In a fight, river crabs lock pincers and push against each other. The winner is the crab that overturns its opponent.

Crabs of the same kind often live close to each other, but competition for food means that each has its own patch of territory to defend. Actual fighting is very risky, because an injured crab is more likely to be caught by a predator, so signals are usually used to solve these conflicts. If this fails and a neighbor comes too close, a fight may ensue. Limbs may be lost during fights, or the protective carapace cracked. Smaller individuals are even killed —and eaten by the winner!

These Sally Lightfoot crabs are fighting with each trying to damage the other with their pincers. Unless one backs down, even the winner may suffer a serious injury.

Land crabs may gather together in large "armies" while they are foraging. When the young adult land crabs first emerge from the sea, larger adults are often waiting—to eat them!

allowed to go where they want, even into the territory of other crabs. A smaller male or female will not risk injury or death by challenging a larger trespasser.

SIGNALS

If a face-to-face encounter between two crabs occurs, then the smaller crab usually backs off rather than risk injury. But if two well-matched crabs meet up, things are carried a stage further. The two crabs start to signal to each other by raising a pair of walking legs. Sometimes a signaling crab raises itself up onto its feet in order to make itself look larger and more fierce. The next stage is more aggressive. Each waves its chelipeds. If this exchange of signals does not sort out which crab is the victor, then the crabs start to push or barge into each other and may take hold of each other with their pincers. Even then, one crab usually retreats before any damage is done.

Some kinds of crabs prefer to seek safety in numbers, so they get together in large groups. The idea is that if you are the only crab around, a crab-eating predator will surely get you, but if you are one of hundreds of crabs, then there is a good chance that your neighbor will be eaten, and not you!

Some crabs even have a kind of social structure. This is usually determined by size and strength. The largest, strongest crabs are most often males, and they are

TERRITORY

Many of the crabs that spend some or most of their time on land have a territory that each defends against intruders. These crabs need a burrow in which to shelter and keep cool. Often the patch of ground surrounding their burrow is their own foraging area. An intruder would therefore be a threat to both their home and their food supply.

This mud crab is sending a very clear message. With its widespread chelipeds and open claws, it is threatening an attack if the intruder approaches more closely.

COMMUNITY CARE

Crabs are vulnerable to predators, especially when they are small or when they have just molted. Half-grown crabs of some marine species gather together to make enormous heaps of crabs. Spider crabs make heaps with the smaller crabs, surrounded by large male crabs.

Waving

Male fiddler crabs have one normal-sized pair of pincers and one huge pair. This large pair is of no use at all for feeding. Instead it has another function. The male fiddler crab uses his one enormous claw to send signals to all the other fiddler crabs around. Fiddler crabs live on tidal mudflats in tropical areas. At low tide, males stand on the heaps of mud by the entrance to their burrows. Then the display begins, with each waving his one huge pair of pincers. They do this to demonstrate ownership of their territory, to threaten rivals and wandering intruders, and to attract females.

This is thought to protect females and young crabs from predators such as octopuses or lobsters. Young Alaskan king crabs also pile up on top of each other. Then they spread out into a huge army of crabs that look for food together over the seabed.

CHAPTER 6
Reproduction

 Male crabs are often bigger and have larger claws than females.

 A female crab carrying her eggs is said to be "in berry."

 The edible crab lays up to 3 million eggs in a batch!

 A freshly laid crab's egg is tiny —most are about one-hundredth of an inch (0.3 mm) across, but they swell a bit as they develop.

 When a land crab's eggs are about to hatch, the female has to walk back to the sea to release them.

Male and female crabs have to overcome any urge to fight each other if they are to pair up and mate. When a female crab is ready to mate, she gives out signals that the male crab can recognize. Female crabs that live in the water often produce special chemicals that males pick up and follow. When they meet, a male and female may use special signs or touch each other with their antennae to let each other know that they are not going to attack.

Swimming crabs mate just after the female has molted. This velvet swimming crab male will go on holding his mate until her new shell has hardened.

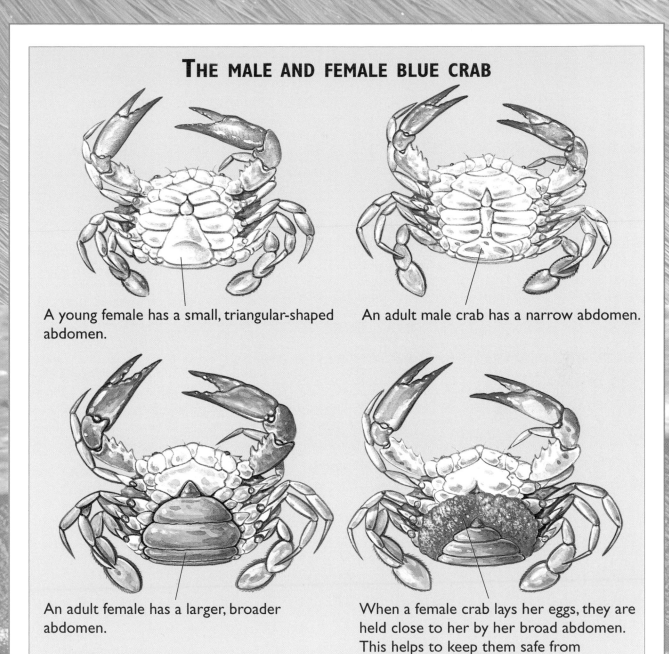

THE MALE AND FEMALE BLUE CRAB

A young female has a small, triangular-shaped abdomen.

An adult male crab has a narrow abdomen.

An adult female has a larger, broader abdomen.

When a female crab lays her eggs, they are held close to her by her broad abdomen. This helps to keep them safe from predators that would eat the eggs.

A female crab has a broader abdomen than the male, and it is fringed with eight small limb-like structures. After she has mated, eggs develop inside her body until they are ready to be laid in one egg mass. She holds this mass of eggs under her body, kept in place by her flap-like abdomen and clasped by the tiny limbs, until they are ready to hatch. Some crabs may produce two batches of eggs a year, others up to six. Each batch contains thousands of tiny eggs.

COURTING

Some male crabs do not make very attentive suitors and have the briefest of courtships. A female hermit crab is quickly grabbed by a male, or many males if she is outnumbered. If a larger female hermit is spotted, the males abandon the smaller female because a larger female will be able to produce and carry more eggs.

By contrast, other male crabs seem to be more caring. Male burrowing crabs, shore crabs, and some swimming crabs carry the female around for a few days before mating. They mate just after the female has molted. The male then continues to carry her around and

This female shore crab is "in berry" and will carry her eggs around from 12 to 18 weeks until they hatch.

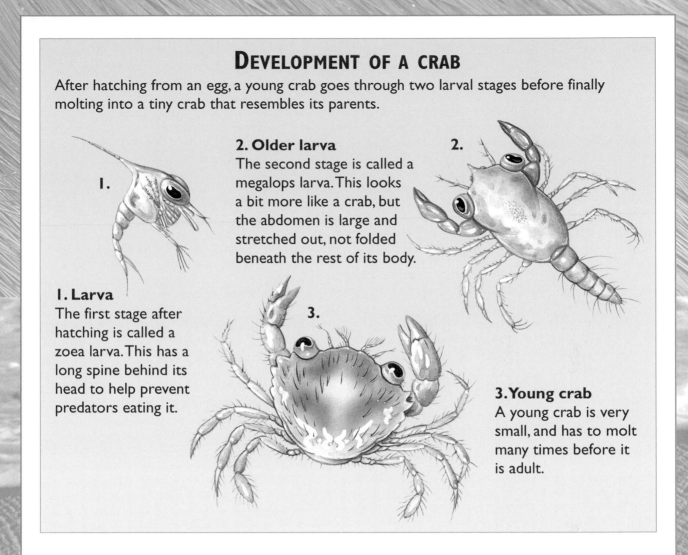

DEVELOPMENT OF A CRAB

After hatching from an egg, a young crab goes through two larval stages before finally molting into a tiny crab that resembles its parents.

1.

2. Older larva
The second stage is called a megalops larva. This looks a bit more like a crab, but the abdomen is large and stretched out, not folded beneath the rest of its body.

2.

1. Larva
The first stage after hatching is called a zoea larva. This has a long spine behind its head to help prevent predators eating it.

3.

3. Young crab
A young crab is very small, and has to molt many times before it is adult.

protect her until her new shell has hardened. This also stops other males from mating with her.

HATCHING

Most young crabs do not look at all like their parents. They hatch out as tiny larvae that mostly live among shoals of other tiny animals in the sea, swimming near the surface and feeding on even smaller living organisms. At first, the larva looks a little bit like a tiny shrimp. They do not have any claw-bearing chelipeds or walking legs. After two to four molts, they enter a new stage. This older larva has chelipeds and walking legs, but it looks more like a tiny lobster than a crab. It soon sinks to the seabed, where it walks about for a while before finally molting into a tiny young crab. It will usually be many weeks before a newly hatched larva finally becomes a tiny crab.

MOLTING

The crab's hard cuticle does not stretch. From time to time, a crab has to molt in order to grow larger. Young crabs molt more often than older crabs. Because they are soft and defenseless for some days after molting, this is a dangerous time in the life of a crab, so it hides away somewhere safe.

During molting, the old cuticle splits along a line under each side of the carapace, and the crab wriggles out backwards, pulling its legs out of the old cuticle. The new

This shore crab has recently molted. Its old, discarded shell is lying beside it. The crab has almost doubled in size.

cuticle is very soft. The crab cannot walk because its legs will not support its weight, and it cannot eat. The crab takes up water and expands, stretching its new skin. After about 32 to 60 hours, the crab is able to walk, but it may be another three to seven days before it starts to eat again. The new shell of a large crab may take several weeks to become as hard as the old one.

Loss of a Limb

Limbs may be bitten off in a fight with a rival crab, or while a crab is trying to escape from a predator. Some crabs may actually shed a limb if it is grasped. When a limb is lost or shed, a new one starts to grow as a tiny bud almost immediately. As it regrows, it triggers molting. After two molts, the new limb will be as large as the original.

Bromeliad Crab

Bromeliads are plants of the pineapple family. They grow in tropical American rain forests, where many kinds perch on the boughs of the tall, rain forest trees. The bases of their large, stiff leaves wrap around each other to make a trap for rainwater. High up in the tree tops, the tiny bromeliad crab lives in these "tanks" of water, where the female lays up to 100 large yolky eggs. After they hatch, young crabs develop from the larvae after only six days.

I DIDN'T KNOW THAT

CHAPTER 7
Self-Defense

 Porcelain crabs shed pincers that continue to snap!

 A king crab relies on its armor and strength to ward off predators.

 When danger threatens, a hermit crab withdraws into its shell and blocks the entrance with its right claw, which is larger than the left claw.

 The common hermit crab may put as many as three stinging Calliactis anemones on its shell.

 Deep-sea hermit crabs carry phosphorescent anemones on their shells so they can see in the dark!

With a good pair of pincers on each cheliped, crabs already have handy weapons with which to deter predators, including inquisitive people. A crab's claws can pinch really hard and be very painful. You have to be very careful how you pick up a crab, especially a powerful one, such as the Dungeness crab! A mangrove crab has another trick to play. It pinches its attacker and then sheds its cheliped, which does not let go. While the victim tries to remove the painful pincer, the crab scuttles away and escapes.

The boxer crab holds a sea anemone in each claw. It uses these as stinging weapons when danger threatens, by brandishing the anemones at the predator.

Like a zebra, Adam's urchin crab has black and white stripes. It lives among the long striped spines of a venomous sea urchin, where its stripes make it hard to see.

Many animals find crabs so tasty that they have learned how to avoid the pincers, so crabs have developed other ways of defending themselves. Some simply rely on not being noticed by a hungry predator. They are colored or patterned to match their background. Others have formed curious but fascinating partnerships with very different kinds of sea animals. In many cases, both partners benefit from this teamwork. In others the relationship seems a bit one-sided.

CAMOUFLAGE

Many crabs blend in perfectly with their background. This kind of disguise is called camouflage. As long as they keep still, it can be difficult to make out their shape. Hairy wharf crabs have tufts of hairs on their legs and back. These crabs live on the seabed, where sand and silt gets trapped among these tufts, making these crabs look just like sandy pebbles.

Others take camouflage a step further. Spider crabs plant fragments of seaweed and sponges among the hooked hairs on their rough carapaces, and some settle there naturally. This makes a spider crab look just like a seaweed-covered rock, but the spider crab has to replace its camouflage every time it molts. Sponge crabs search around for the sea-orange sponge. They break off a small piece of this sponge and hold it against their carapace with their last pair of walking legs. This sponge grows right over the crab's carapace in an orange-yellow dome. Tucked away underneath, the crab is completely invisible.

CURIOUS PARTNERSHIPS

There are many partnerships between sea anemones and crabs. The crabs benefit partly because the anemones help to disguise the crabs, and partly because the tentacles of sea anemones are full of stinging cells that help to keep predators away. The anemones benefit because they feed on fragments of food stirred up from the sea bed as the crab moves around.

This hermit crab has two stinging anemones on its shell. The hermit crab gains protection from predators. The anemones get a supply of food particles from the hermit's prey and from the seabed as the crab walks around.

The cloak anemone lives with a small hermit crab that is only about 2 inches (5 cm) long when it is full-grown. When the crab is young, it is small enough to live inside a little winkle shell. Instead of perching on the top of the shell, the cloak anemone settles underneath. It grows up and right over the winkle shell, completely covering it. Then it grows out over the opening, to make a tube. The hermit crab and the anemone grow larger together, so the crab never needs to find a larger shell in which to live.

Pea Crabs

Tiny pea crabs protect themselves by living inside the shell of a living mollusk, such as a mussel. The pea crab gets a safe home inside the thick shell of the mollusk, and it gets something else as well—a food supply. Mollusks feed by straining tiny organisms and floating particles from a current of sea water that they draw into their shell and over their gills. Particles of food are trapped in slimy mucus, and the pea crab helps itself whenever it is hungry.

I DIDN'T KNOW THAT

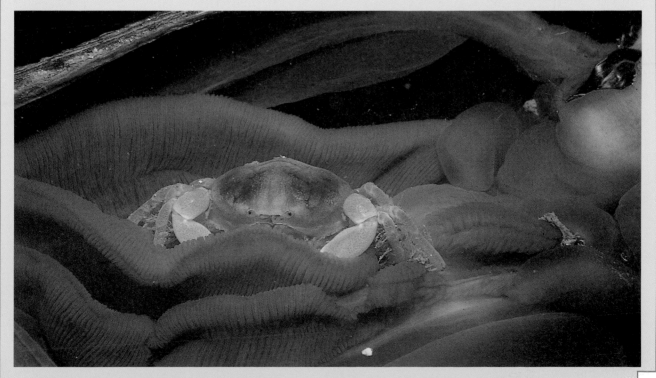

CHAPTER 8
Threats and Enemies

 The Australian crab lives for only one year.

 The edible crab may live as long as 20 years.

 Detergents used in the 1960s to clean up oil spills at sea caused contaminated crabs to lose their legs.

Crabs have many natural enemies. There are plenty of predatory animals that will catch and eat them. These include seabirds, otters, raccoons, wild cats, and foxes, especially the crab-eating fox of eastern South America. People also enjoy eating crabs. For many people all around the world, crabs are a special treat. For others, they are a valuable source of protein.

Unfortunately, just like many other marine animals that people enjoy eating, some kinds of large crabs are in danger from overfishing. Although female crabs lay truly

Large numbers of commercially valuable crabs, like these Dungeness crabs, are taken by fishers every year.

A sea otter swims slowly along on its back as it cracks open a crab to get at the nutritious flesh inside.

enormous numbers of eggs, most of the larval crabs and tiny young crabs are eaten by hungry predators. The edible and Dungeness crabs reproduce before they are full-grown, but these smaller crabs are still more vulnerable than their full-grown relatives. It may take many years for them to reach full size, so if too many are taken by crab fishers, the remaining population may fall to a dangerously low level, threatening the species' survival.

Another threat, especially to the kinds of crabs that live in estuaries and in shallow coastal regions, comes from pollution. Sewage from towns and settlements near the coast is often allowed to flow into the sea.

Agriculture and industries also discharge some of their waste products into rivers and the sea. These outflows all cause changes to the water quality. Often they also introduce poisonous chemicals into streams, rivers, lakes, and oceans.

CRAB FISHING

Crabs are caught in the sea by trapping or netting. Crab traps are rather like baskets with an entrance that is easy for the crabs to walk into but from which it is not easy for a crab to escape.

These traps are baited with fish heads or chicken parts. Different kinds of crabs are taken, such as the Dungeness crab along the western coast of the United States and the edible crab in European waters. Nets are used to catch swimming crabs in southeast Asian seas, and Japanese and Russian fishers also use tangle nets to catch king crabs and tanner crabs. The blue crab from the eastern coast of the United States is the mainstay of the soft-shell crab industry. These crabs are caught and eaten shortly after molting, before their new cuticle has hardened. Because overfishing threatened the survival of this species, laws have been introduced in many places making it illegal to catch blue crabs under a certain size. It is also illegal to capture and keep a female blue crab carrying her eggs.

HUNGRY PREDATORS

In the sea, fish and octopuses feed greedily on crabs. Along the shore and in tide pools, seagulls and crows hunt for them. Land crabs are eaten by many mammals, especially foxes and raccoons,

A collared kingfisher from Indonesia is just one of many kinds of birds that regularly catch and eat crabs, and feed them to their chicks.

but in fact most animals will eat land crabs if given the chance. Around the shores of Scotland, otters catch crabs living among the seaweed, taking them out onto exposed rocks before cracking their shells with their teeth and eating the flesh. In

A crab's hard shell is no defense against a hungry giant octopus. The octopus cracks open the shell with its hard, beaklike mouthparts.

Africa, the giant water shrew is particularly fond of crabs and may eat as many as 25 freshwater crabs in one night.

Pollution

When gigantic oil tankers get wrecked on rocks or damaged by storms, enormous amounts of oil may pour into the sea. In a major oil spill, such as the *Exxon Valdez* disaster of 1989, immediate public concern is for those birds that are so clearly harmed or killed by the oil. The precise effect such a spill has on shellfish and crustaceans is often not known, yet it is certain that such disasters can have a serious impact on crab populations and local diversity.

UNWANTED ALIENS

In any environment, there is a balance among the animals that occupy it. This balance can be upset if a new species is introduced. For instance, the green crab is naturally found near the shorelines of western and southern Europe. It has been introduced to North American shores, where it competes with the native Dungeness crab, both by eating its prey and by eating the Dungeness crab itself. It is also affecting clam, oyster, and crab fisheries.

The green crab is part of a balanced community in its native environment, but is seriously affecting the populations of Dungeness crabs in its adopted North American home.

The Chinese mitten crab was an accidental introduction to the River Thames estuary in England. This crab can live in fresh water. People are worried that if it flourishes in its new home, the burrows it makes will damage the riverbanks. It is often not a good idea to introduce an alien species into a new environment.

Glossary

ABDOMEN – The part of an animal that usually contains the gut, reproductive and other organs, but which in true crabs, is a thin flap folded against the underside of the thorax

ANTENNAE – Sensitive feelers that a crab uses to detect smells and to feel objects

ARTHROPODS – Invertebrate animals that have a tough outer layer called a cuticle, or exoskeleton, and jointed legs

CAMOUFLAGE – Colors or patterns that allow an animal to blend in with its background

CARAPACE – The hard shell covering the crab's head and thorax

CARNIVORES – Animals that eat mainly the flesh of other animals

CHELIPEDS – The first pair of legs on a crab's thorax, each of which bears a pair of pincers, or claws

COLONY – A large number of animals of the same species, living closely together

COMPOUND EYES – The eye of a crab or insect that is made up of thousands of tiny units, each with its own lens

CRUSTACEANS – Animals such as crabs, lobsters, shrimps, prawns, and barnacles

CUTICLE – The tough outer layer, or exoskeleton, of an arthropod that supports and protects the body within it

EXOSKELETON – The hard outer layer of cuticle that covers all arthropods

FILTER FEEDING – A way in which some marine animals get their food by straining tiny animals and floating particles from the water

GILL CHAMBER – A space surrounding a crab's gills through which water is pumped

GILLS – Feathery structures that absorb dissolved oxygen from sea water

INVERTEBRATES – Animals that do not have a backbone

LARVA – A stage in the life cycle of an animal that hatches from an egg but which does not look like its adult parents

MOLLUSKS – Animals such as slugs, snails, mussels, clams, and oysters

MOLT – To shed the entire outer layer of skin or cuticle

OMNIVORES – Animals that have a wide range of food items in their diet and will eat almost anything, whether plant or animal

OVERFISHING – When a marine animal is gathered or fished in such large quantities that the survival of that species in a particular area becomes endangered

PINCERS – Pairs of claws that pinch, grip, or cut

POLLUTION – Contamination of the environment with substances that are harmful to life

PREDATOR – An animal that hunts another animal for food

PREY – An animal that is caught and eaten by another animal

SCAVENGING – Finding food by foraging or searching among dead or decaying matter, either animal or plant

SPECIES – A kind or type of living organism

TERRITORY – The area that an animal occupies and defends against others of its own kind

THORAX – The part of the body between the head and abdomen

Further Reading

Dunlap, Julie. *Extraordinary Horseshoe Crabs*. Minneapolis: Lerner, 1998.

Johnson, Sylvia A. *Crab*. Minneapolis: Lerner, 1992.

Nathan, Emma. *What Do You Call A Baby Crab? And Other Ocean Animals*. Woodbridge, CT: Blackbirch, 1999.

Tibbits, Christiane K. *Seashells, Crabs, and Sea Stars*. Minnetonka, MN: Creative Publishing, 1996.

Web sites:

Crustacean Society

www.lam.mus.ca.us

Maintained by the Los Angeles County Museum, this site provides articles, photographs, information, and links pertaining to all manner of crustaceans, including crabs.

Acknowledgments

Front cover: Fred Bruemmer/Bruce Coleman Collection; p.8: Orion Press/Bruce Coleman Collection; p.9: G.I.Bernard/Oxford Scientific Films; p.10: Jeff Foot/Bruce Coleman Collection; p.11: B.Jones & M.Shimlock/Natural History Photographic Agency; p.12: Bruce Coleman Collection; p.13: B.Jones & M.Shimlock/Natural History Photographic Agency; p.14: John Cancalosi/Bruce Coleman Collection; p.15 top: A.N.T./Natural History Photographic Agency; p.15 bottom: G.I.Bernard/Oxford Scientific Films; p.16: Kevin Cullimore/Bruce Coleman Collection; p.17: K.G.Preston-Mafham/Premaphotos; p.19: Jane Burton/Bruce Coleman Collection; p.20: Paul Kay/Oxford Scientific Films; p. 21: Animals Animals/Oxford Scientific Films; p.22: K.G.Preston-Mafham/Premaphotos; p.23: K.G.Preston-Mafham/Premaphotos; p.24: Karl Switak/Natural History Photographic Agency; p.25: Richard Herrman/Oxford Scientific Films; p.26: Anthony Bannister/Natural History Photographic Agency; p.27: John Pontier/Animals Animals/Oxford Scientific Films; p.28: Andrew Purcell/Bruce Coleman Collection; p.30: Jane Burton/Bruce Coleman Collection; p.32: Dr Rod Preston-Mafham/Premaphotos; p.34: B.Jones & M.Shimlock/Natural History Photographic Agency; p.35: B.Jones & M.Shimlock/Natural History Photographic Agency; p.36: Yves Lanceau/Natural History Photographic Agency; p.37: Karen Gowlett-Holmes/Oxford Scientific Films; p.38: John Cancalosi/Bruce Coleman Collection; p.39: Jeff Foott/Bruce Coleman Collection; p.40: Mary Plage./Bruce Coleman Collection; p.41: Mark Deeble & Victoria Stone/Oxford Scientific Films; p.42: Andrew Davies/Bruce Coleman Collection; p.43: Dr Rod Preston-Mafham/Premaphotos.

Index